Daily
Prayer
Journal

BARBOUR
PUBLISHING, INC.
Uhrichsville, Ohio

© MCMLXXXVI by Barbour Publishing, Inc.

ISBN 0-916441-61-X

All Scripture is taken from the King James Version of the Bible.

Published by Barbour Publishing, Inc.
P.O. Box 719
Uhrichsville, Ohio 44683
http://www.barbourbooks.com

 Member of the
Evangelical Christian
Publishers Association

Printed in the United States of America.

January 1

"Seek ye first the kingdom of God, and his righteousness, and all these things shall be added unto you."

Matthew 6:33

_____

_____

_____

_____

_____

_____

_____

_____

_____

_____

_____

_____

_____

_____

_____

_____

_____

_____

_____

January 2

"Evening, and morning, and at noon, will I pray, and cry aloud, and he shall hear my voice."

Psalm 55:17

_____
_____
_____
_____
_____
_____
_____
_____
_____
_____
_____
_____
_____
_____
_____
_____

January 3

"And whatever ye shall ask in my name, that will I do, that the Father may be glorified in the Son."

John 14:13

January 4

*"He hath made every thing
beautiful in its time; . . ."*

Ecclesiastes 3:11

_____

_____

_____

_____

_____

_____

_____

_____

_____

_____

_____

_____

_____

_____

_____

_____

_____

January 5

"Let us hold fast the profession of our faith without wavering (for he is faithful that promised)"

Hebrews 10:23

_____
_____
_____
_____
_____
_____
_____
_____
_____
_____
_____
_____
_____
_____
_____
_____
_____

January 6

"He that handleth a matter wisely shall find good; and whoso trusteth in the Lord, happy is he."

Proverbs 16:20

_____
_____
_____
_____
_____
_____
_____
_____
_____
_____
_____
_____
_____
_____
_____
_____

January 7

"The effectual, fervent prayer of a righteous man availeth much."

James 5:16

January 8

*"Though your sins be as scarlet,
they shall be made white as snow;"*

Isaiah 1:18

_____

_____

_____

_____

_____

_____

_____

_____

_____

_____

_____

_____

_____

_____

_____

_____

January 9

"But if we walk in the light, as he is in the light, we have fellowship one with another," 1 John 1:7

_____
_____
_____
_____
_____
_____
_____
_____
_____
_____
_____
_____
_____
_____
_____
_____
_____
_____

January 10

"Every word of God is pure; he is a shield unto those who put their trust in him."

Proverbs 30:5

_____

_____

_____

_____

_____

_____

_____

_____

_____

_____

_____

_____

_____

_____

_____

_____

_____

January 11

"I will never leave thee, nor forsake thee." *Hebrews 13:5*

January 12

"The Lord is good, a stronghold in the day of trouble, and he knoweth those who trust in him." Nahum 1:7

_____
_____
_____
_____
_____
_____
_____
_____
_____
_____
_____
_____
_____
_____
_____
_____
_____

January 13

"But godliness with contentment is great gain."   *1 Timothy 6:6*

_____

_____

_____

_____

_____

_____

_____

_____

_____

_____

_____

_____

_____

_____

_____

_____

_____

January 14

"For I, the Lord thy God, will hold thy right hand, saying unto thee, Fear not; I will help thee."

Isaiah 41:13

_____
_____
_____
_____
_____
_____
_____
_____
_____
_____
_____
_____
_____
_____
_____
_____
_____

January 15

"If God be for us, who can be against us?" Romans 8:31

_____
_____
_____
_____
_____
_____
_____
_____
_____
_____
_____
_____
_____
_____
_____
_____
_____
_____

January 16

"I will instruct thee and teach thee in the way which thou shalt go."

Psalm 32:8

_____

_____

_____

_____

_____

_____

_____

_____

_____

_____

_____

_____

_____

_____

_____

_____

January 17

"For where two or three are gathered in my name, there am I in the midst of them." *Matthew 18:20*

_____
_____
_____
_____
_____
_____
_____
_____
_____
_____
_____
_____
_____
_____
_____
_____
_____
_____

January 18

"He shall deliver thee in six troubles; yea, in seven there shall no evil touch thee." Job 5:19

January 19

"And ye are Christ's, and Christ is God's."　　　*1 Corinthians 3:23*

_____
_____
_____
_____
_____
_____
_____
_____
_____
_____
_____
_____
_____
_____
_____
_____
_____
_____
_____
_____

January 20

". . . Behold, I will pour out my spirit unto you, I will make known my words unto you." Proverbs 1:23

_____

_____

_____

_____

_____

_____

_____

_____

_____

_____

_____

_____

_____

_____

_____

_____

January 21

"Walk in the Spirit, and ye shall not fulfill the lust of the flesh."

Galatians 5:16

_____

_____

_____

_____

_____

_____

_____

_____

_____

_____

_____

_____

_____

_____

_____

_____

_____

_____

January 22

"The Lord preserveth all those who love him." *Psalm 145:20*

_____
_____
_____
_____
_____
_____
_____
_____
_____
_____
_____
_____
_____
_____
_____
_____
_____
_____
_____
_____

January 23

"And let us not be weary in well doing; for in due season we shall reap, if we faint not." Galatians 6:9

_____

_____

_____

_____

_____

_____

_____

_____

_____

_____

_____

_____

_____

_____

_____

_____

_____

_____

January 24

"And he shall be like a tree planted by the rivers of water." Psalm 1:3

_____
_____
_____
_____
_____
_____
_____
_____
_____
_____
_____
_____
_____
_____
_____
_____
_____
_____
_____

January 25

"He that followeth me shall not walk in darkness, but shall have the light of life."   *John 8:12*

_____
_____
_____
_____
_____
_____
_____
_____
_____
_____
_____
_____
_____
_____
_____
_____
_____
_____

January 26

"Fear thou not; for I am with thee."
Isaiah 41:10

_____

_____

_____

_____

_____

_____

_____

_____

_____

_____

_____

_____

_____

_____

_____

_____

_____

_____

January 27

"We are more than conquerors through him that loved us."

January 28

"The Lord is good unto those who wait for him, to the soul that seeketh him."

Lamentations 3:25

_____
_____
_____
_____
_____
_____
_____
_____
_____
_____
_____
_____
_____
_____
_____
_____
_____

January 29

"To live is Christ, and to die is gain."

Philippians 1:21

_____

_____

_____

_____

_____

_____

_____

_____

_____

_____

_____

_____

_____

_____

_____

_____

_____

_____

January 30

"The Lord executeth righteousness and judgment for all who are oppressed." *Psalm 103:6*

_____

_____

_____

_____

_____

_____

_____

_____

_____

_____

_____

_____

_____

_____

_____

_____

_____

_____

January 31

"Greater is he that is in you, than he that is in the world."

1 John 4:4

_____

_____

_____

_____

_____

_____

_____

_____

_____

_____

_____

_____

_____

_____

_____

_____

_____

February 1

"Blessed is the man who trusteth in the Lord, and whose hope the Lord is."

Jeremiah 17:7

_____
_____
_____
_____
_____
_____
_____
_____
_____
_____
_____
_____
_____
_____
_____
_____
_____
_____
_____
_____

February 2

*". . . And the blood of Jesus Christ,
his Son, cleanseth us from all sin."*

1 John 1:7

_____

_____

_____

_____

_____

_____

_____

_____

_____

_____

_____

_____

_____

_____

_____

_____

_____

February 3

"I will guide thee with mine eye."

Psalm 32:8

_____
_____
_____
_____
_____
_____
_____
_____
_____
_____
_____
_____
_____
_____
_____
_____
_____
_____
_____
_____
_____

February 4

"Behold, I come quickly."

Revelation 22:7

_____
_____
_____
_____
_____
_____
_____
_____
_____
_____
_____
_____
_____
_____
_____
_____
_____
_____
_____
_____

February 5

"I will strengthen thee; yea, I will help thee; yea, I will uphold thee with the right hand of my righteousness."

Isaiah 41:10

_____
_____
_____
_____
_____
_____
_____
_____
_____
_____
_____
_____
_____
_____
_____
_____
_____
_____

February 6

". . . All things work together for good to them that love God,"

Romans 8:28

_____

_____

_____

_____

_____

_____

_____

_____

_____

_____

_____

_____

_____

_____

_____

_____

_____

_____

_____

_____

February 7

"But they that wait upon the Lord shall renew their strength."

Isaiah 40:31

_____

_____

_____

_____

_____

_____

_____

_____

_____

_____

_____

_____

_____

_____

_____

_____

_____

_____

February 8

"And I give unto them eternal life; and they shall never perish, neither shall any man pluck them out of my hand."

John 10:28

February 9

"The Lord of hosts is with us; the God of Jacob is our refuge."

Psalm 46:11

_____
_____
_____
_____
_____
_____
_____
_____
_____
_____
_____
_____
_____
_____
_____
_____

February 10

"He that soweth to the Spirit shall of the Spirit reap life everlasting."

Galatians 6:8

_____
_____
_____
_____
_____
_____
_____
_____
_____
_____
_____
_____
_____
_____
_____
_____
_____
_____
_____

February 11

"He took not away the pillar of the cloud by day, nor the pillar of fire by night, from before the people."

Exodus 13:22

_____

_____

_____

_____

_____

_____

_____

_____

_____

_____

_____

_____

_____

_____

_____

_____

_____

_____

February 12

"My grace is sufficient for thee; for my strength is made perfect in weakness."   *2 Corinthians 12:9*

_____

_____

_____

_____

_____

_____

_____

_____

_____

_____

_____

_____

_____

_____

_____

_____

_____

_____

February 13

"I will pour water upon him that is thirsty, and floods upon the dry ground."   *Isaiah 44:3*

_____
_____
_____
_____
_____
_____
_____
_____
_____
_____
_____
_____
_____
_____
_____
_____
_____

February 14

". . . And everyone that loveth is born of God, and knoweth God."

1 John 4:7

February 15

"He giveth power to the faint; and to those who have no might he increaseth strength."   Isaiah 40:29

_____
_____
_____
_____
_____
_____
_____
_____
_____
_____
_____
_____
_____
_____
_____
_____
_____

February 16

"Grace and peace be multiplied unto you through the knowledge of God, and of Jesus, our Lord."

1 Peter 1:2

_____
_____
_____
_____
_____
_____
_____
_____
_____
_____
_____
_____
_____
_____
_____
_____
_____
_____

February 17

"Call upon me in the day of trouble: I will deliver thee, and thou shalt glorify Me." *Psalm 50:15*

_____
_____
_____
_____
_____
_____
_____
_____
_____
_____
_____
_____
_____
_____
_____
_____
_____

February 18

"And being fully persuaded that, what he had promised, he was able also to perform." Romans 4:21

_____
_____
_____
_____
_____
_____
_____
_____
_____
_____
_____
_____
_____
_____
_____
_____
_____

February 19

"The Lord shall preserve thee from all evil; He shall preserve thy soul."

Psalm 121:7

_____
_____
_____
_____
_____
_____
_____
_____
_____
_____
_____
_____
_____
_____
_____
_____
_____
_____

February 20

"And I will give unto thee the keys of the kingdom of heaven."

Matthew 16:19

_____
_____
_____
_____
_____
_____
_____
_____
_____
_____
_____
_____
_____
_____
_____
_____
_____
_____
_____

February 21

"Ye shall not be afraid of the face of man; for the judgment is God's."

Deuteronomy 1:17

_____

_____

_____

_____

_____

_____

_____

_____

_____

_____

_____

_____

_____

_____

_____

_____

February 22

"I will give unto him that is athirst of the fountain of the water of life freely."

Revelation 21:6

February 23

"Those that be planted in the house of the Lord shall flourish in the courts of our God."   *Psalm 92:13*

_____
_____
_____
_____
_____
_____
_____
_____
_____
_____
_____
_____
_____
_____
_____
_____
_____
_____
_____

February 24

"For my yoke is easy, and my burden is light." *Matthew 11:30*

_____

_____

_____

_____

_____

_____

_____

_____

_____

_____

_____

_____

_____

_____

_____

_____

_____

_____

February 25

". . . the Lord will hear when I call unto Him."   *Psalm 4:3*

_____

_____

_____

_____

_____

_____

_____

_____

_____

_____

_____

_____

_____

_____

_____

_____

_____

February 26

"And God is able to make all grace abound toward you,"

2 Corinthians 9:8

_____
_____
_____
_____
_____
_____
_____
_____
_____
_____
_____
_____
_____
_____
_____
_____
_____
_____
_____

February 27

"He shall feed his flock like a shepherd."

Isaiah 40:11

_____
_____
_____
_____
_____
_____
_____
_____
_____
_____
_____
_____
_____
_____
_____
_____
_____
_____

February 28

"Come after me, and I will make you become fishers of men."

Mark 1:17

_____

_____

_____

_____

_____

_____

_____

_____

_____

_____

_____

_____

_____

_____

_____

_____

_____

_____

February 29

"For thou wilt light my candle; the Lord, my God, will lighten my darkness."

Psalm 18:28

March 1

"The desire of the righteous shall be granted." — Proverbs 10:24

March 2

"Let us therefore come boldly unto the throne of grace, that we may obtain mercy . . ." Hebrews 4:16

_____
_____
_____
_____
_____
_____
_____
_____
_____
_____
_____
_____
_____
_____
_____
_____
_____

March 3

"The young lions do lack, and suffer hunger; but they who seek the Lord shall not want any good thing."

Psalm 34:10

_____
_____
_____
_____
_____
_____
_____
_____
_____
_____
_____
_____
_____
_____
_____
_____
_____
_____

March 4

". . . Thy Father, who seeth in secret, himself shall reward thee openly."   Matthew 6:4

_____

_____

_____

_____

_____

_____

_____

_____

_____

_____

_____

_____

_____

_____

_____

_____

_____

March 5

"Though our outward man perish, yet the inward man is renewed day by day."
1 Corinthians 4:16

_____
_____
_____
_____
_____
_____
_____
_____
_____
_____
_____
_____
_____
_____
_____
_____
_____
_____
_____
_____

March 6

". . . He that dwelleth in love dwelleth in God, and God in him."

1 John 4:16

_____
_____
_____
_____
_____
_____
_____
_____
_____
_____
_____
_____
_____
_____
_____
_____
_____
_____
_____

March 7

"I will be with him in trouble; I will deliver him and honor him."

Psalm 91:15

March 8

"For our light affliction, which is but for a moment, worketh for us a far more exceeding and eternal weight of glory."

2 Corinthians 4:17

_____

_____

_____

_____

_____

_____

_____

_____

_____

_____

_____

_____

_____

_____

_____

_____

_____

_____

March 9

"Great is thy faithfulness"

Lamentations 3:23

_____

_____

_____

_____

_____

_____

_____

_____

_____

_____

_____

_____

_____

_____

_____

_____

_____

_____

_____

March 10

*"Above all, taking the shield of faith,
wherewith ye shall be able to quench all
the fiery darts of the wicked."*

Ephesians 6:16

_____
_____
_____
_____
_____
_____
_____
_____
_____
_____
_____
_____
_____
_____
_____
_____
_____
_____

March 11

"Hath he said, and shall he not do it? or hath He spoken, and shall He not make it good?"   Numbers 23:19

March 12

"Behold, I shew you a mystery; we shall not all sleep, but we shall all be changed."   *1 Corinthians 15:51*

_____

_____

_____

_____

_____

_____

_____

_____

_____

_____

_____

_____

_____

_____

_____

_____

_____

March 13

"Then will I hear from heaven, and will forgive their sin, and will heal their land."   2 Chronicles 7:14

_____

_____

_____

_____

_____

_____

_____

_____

_____

_____

_____

_____

_____

_____

_____

_____

_____

March 14

*"And there shall be no night there . . .
for the Lord God giveth them light, and
they shall reign forever and ever."*

Revelations 22:5

_____
_____
_____
_____
_____
_____
_____
_____
_____
_____
_____
_____
_____
_____
_____
_____
_____

March 15

"The Lord is nigh unto all them that call upon Him, to all that call upon Him in truth."   *Psalm 145:18*

_____
_____
_____
_____
_____
_____
_____
_____
_____
_____
_____
_____
_____
_____
_____
_____
_____
_____

March 16

"And as we have borne the image of the earthy, we shall also bear the image of the heavenly."

1 Corinthians 15:49

_____
_____
_____
_____
_____
_____
_____
_____
_____
_____
_____
_____
_____
_____
_____
_____
_____

March 17

"My defense is of God, which saveth the upright in heart."

Psalm 7:10

March 18

*"He that loveth his brother abideth
in the light . . ."*   *1 John 2:10*

_____
_____
_____
_____
_____
_____
_____
_____
_____
_____
_____
_____
_____
_____
_____
_____
_____

March 19

"The Lord shall preserve thy going out and thy coming in from this time forth and even forevermore."

Psalm 121:8

_____

_____

_____

_____

_____

_____

_____

_____

_____

_____

_____

_____

_____

_____

_____

_____

_____

March 20

"For in that He Himself hath suffered being tempted, He is able to succour them that are tempted."

Hebrews 2:18

_____
_____
_____
_____
_____
_____
_____
_____
_____
_____
_____
_____
_____
_____
_____
_____
_____

March 21

"And ye shall seek Me, and find Me, when ye shall search for Me with all your heart." *Jeremiah 29:13*

_____
_____
_____
_____
_____
_____
_____
_____
_____
_____
_____
_____
_____
_____
_____
_____
_____
_____

March 22

"For whosoever shall call upon the name of the Lord shall be saved."

Romans 10:13

_____

_____

_____

_____

_____

_____

_____

_____

_____

_____

_____

_____

_____

_____

_____

March 23

"He will not suffer thy foot to be moved; He who keepeth thee will not slumber."   *Psalm 121:3*

_____

_____

_____

_____

_____

_____

_____

_____

_____

_____

_____

_____

_____

_____

_____

_____

_____

March 24

"For God hath not appointed us to wrath, but to obtain salvation by our Lord Jesus Christ."

1 Thessalonians 5:9

March 25

". . . my kindness shall not depart from thee . . . saith the Lord, who hath mercy on thee."   *Isaiah 54:10*

_____

_____

_____

_____

_____

_____

_____

_____

_____

_____

_____

_____

_____

_____

_____

_____

_____

_____

March 26

"And this I pray, that your love may abound yet more and more in knowledge and in all judgment."

Philippians 1:9

March 27

"I will dwell in the midst of thee."
Zechariah 2:11

_____
_____
_____
_____
_____
_____
_____
_____
_____
_____
_____
_____
_____
_____
_____
_____
_____
_____
_____
_____

March 28

"Blessed are the pure in heart; for they shall see God."   Matthew 5:8

_____

_____

_____

_____

_____

_____

_____

_____

_____

_____

_____

_____

_____

_____

_____

_____

_____

_____

March 29

"Commit thy way unto the Lord; trust also in him; and he shall bring it to pass."   *Psalm 37:5*

_____

_____

_____

_____

_____

_____

_____

_____

_____

_____

_____

_____

_____

_____

_____

_____

_____

March 30

"The Spirit itself beareth witness with our spirit, that we are the children of God."   Romans 8:16

_____
_____
_____
_____
_____
_____
_____
_____
_____
_____
_____
_____
_____
_____
_____
_____
_____
_____

March 31

"I will even make a way in the wilderness, and rivers in the desert." *Isaiah 43:19*

_____

_____

_____

_____

_____

_____

_____

_____

_____

_____

_____

_____

_____

_____

_____

_____

_____

_____

April 1

"For the Lord Himself shall descend from heaven, with a shout . . . and the dead in Christ shall rise first."

1 Thessalonians 4:16

_____

_____

_____

_____

_____

_____

_____

_____

_____

_____

_____

_____

_____

_____

_____

_____

_____

April 2

"He shall call upon Me and I will answer him . . ."   *Psalm 91:15*

_____

_____

_____

_____

_____

_____

_____

_____

_____

_____

_____

_____

_____

_____

_____

_____

_____

_____

April 3

"I am the resurrection, and the Life; he that believeth in Me, though he were dead, yet shall he live."

John 11:25

_____

_____

_____

_____

_____

_____

_____

_____

_____

_____

_____

_____

_____

_____

_____

_____

April 4

"Call unto me, and I will answer thee, and shew thee great and mighty things." *Jeremiah 33:3*

_____
_____
_____
_____
_____
_____
_____
_____
_____
_____
_____
_____
_____
_____
_____
_____
_____
_____

April 5

"Now thanks be unto God, who always causeth us to triumph in Christ."

2 Corinthians 2:14

April 6

"I will bless the Lord, who hath given me counsel." *Psalm 16:7*

_____

_____

_____

_____

_____

_____

_____

_____

_____

_____

_____

_____

_____

_____

_____

_____

_____

_____

April 7

"For the eyes of the Lord are over the righteous and His ears are open unto their prayers."   *1 Peter 3:12*

_____
_____
_____
_____
_____
_____
_____
_____
_____
_____
_____
_____
_____
_____
_____
_____
_____
_____
_____

April 8

"No weapon that is formed against thee shall prosper."　　*Isaiah 54:17*

_____
_____
_____
_____
_____
_____
_____
_____
_____
_____
_____
_____
_____
_____
_____
_____
_____
_____
_____
_____

April 9

"For God so loved the world, that he gave his only begotten Son, that whosoever believeth in him should . . . have everlasting life." John 3:16

April 10

"Blessed are they that keep his testimonies, and that seek Him with the whole heart." Psalm 119:2

_____

_____

_____

_____

_____

_____

_____

_____

_____

_____

_____

_____

_____

_____

_____

_____

_____

_____

_____

April 11

"Blessed are the peacemakers: for they shall be called the children of God."
                                        Matthew 5:9

_____
_____
_____
_____
_____
_____
_____
_____
_____
_____
_____
_____
_____
_____
_____
_____
_____

April 12

"But if from thence thou shalt seek the Lord thy God, thou shalt find Him."

Deuteronomy 4:29

_____

_____

_____

_____

_____

_____

_____

_____

_____

_____

_____

_____

_____

_____

_____

_____

_____

April 13

*"So then faith cometh by hearing;
and hearing by the word of God."*

Romans 10:17

_____
_____
_____
_____
_____
_____
_____
_____
_____
_____
_____
_____
_____
_____
_____
_____
_____
_____

April 14

*"Weeping may endure for a night,
but joy cometh in the morning."*

Psalm 30:5

_____

_____

_____

_____

_____

_____

_____

_____

_____

_____

_____

_____

_____

_____

_____

_____

_____

April 15

"For if our heart condemn us, God is greater than our heart, and knoweth all things . . ."   1 John 3:20

_____

_____

_____

_____

_____

_____

_____

_____

_____

_____

_____

_____

_____

_____

_____

_____

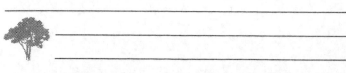

_____

_____

April 16

"I send an angel before thee, to keep thee in the way, and to bring thee into the place which I have prepared."

Exodus 23:20

_____
_____
_____
_____
_____
_____
_____
_____
_____
_____
_____
_____
_____
_____
_____
_____
_____
_____
_____

April 17

"Every good and perfect gift is from above, and cometh down from the Father of lights,"

James 1:17

_____
_____
_____
_____
_____
_____
_____
_____
_____
_____
_____
_____
_____
_____
_____
_____

April 18

"For them that honor me I will honor . . ." 1 Samuel 2:30

_____

_____

_____

_____

_____

_____

_____

_____

_____

_____

_____

_____

_____

_____

_____

_____

_____

_____

_____

April 19

"For the word of God is quick, and powerful, and sharper than any two-edged sword." *Hebrews 4:12*

_____

_____

_____

_____

_____

_____

_____

_____

_____

_____

_____

_____

_____

_____

_____

_____

April 20

"As for God, His way is perfect."

Psalm 18:30

_____
_____
_____
_____
_____
_____
_____
_____
_____
_____
_____
_____
_____
_____
_____
_____
_____
_____
_____

April 21

"And you hath he quickened, who were dead in trespasses and sins; . . ."   *Ephesians 2:1*

_____

_____

_____

_____

_____

_____

_____

_____

_____

_____

_____

_____

_____

_____

_____

_____

April 22

"Understand, therefore, this day, that the Lord thy God is He who goeth over before thee;"

Deuteronomy 9:3

April 23

"For God hath not given us the spirit of fear; but of power, and of love, and of a sound mind."

2 Timothy 1:7

April 24

"I will ransom them from the power of the grave; I will redeem them from death."   *Hosea 13:14*

_____
_____
_____
_____
_____
_____
_____
_____
_____
_____
_____
_____
_____
_____
_____
_____
_____
_____

April 25

"For we are His workmanship, created in Christ Jesus unto good works."   *Ephesians 2:10*

April 26

"I will seek that which was lost, and bring again that which was driven away,"   *Ezekiel 34:16*

_____
_____
_____
_____
_____
_____
_____
_____
_____
_____
_____
_____
_____
_____
_____
_____
_____
_____
_____
_____
_____

April 27

"Casting all your care upon Him; for He careth for you."   *1 Peter 5:7*

_____

_____

_____

_____

_____

_____

_____

_____

_____

_____

_____

_____

_____

_____

_____

_____

_____

_____

April 28

"Thy word have I hid in my heart,
that I might not sin against thee."

Psalm 119:11

_____

_____

_____

_____

_____

_____

_____

_____

_____

_____

_____

_____

_____

_____

_____

_____

_____

_____

April 29

"If any of you lack wisdom, let him ask of God, who giveth to all men liberally,"

James 1:5

April 30

"Sorrow is turned into joy before him."

Job 41:22

_____

_____

_____

_____

_____

_____

_____

_____

_____

_____

_____

_____

_____

_____

_____

_____

_____

_____

May 1

"As I was with Moses, so I will be with thee; I will not fail thee, nor forsake thee." Joshua 1:5

May 2

"But my God shall supply all your need according to his riches in glory by Christ Jesus."

Philippians 4:19

_____

_____

_____

_____

_____

_____

_____

_____

_____

_____

_____

_____

_____

_____

_____

_____

_____

_____

May 3

"Thou will keep him in perfect peace, whose mind is stayed on thee . . ."   *Isaiah 26:3*

_____

_____

_____

_____

_____

_____

_____

_____

_____

_____

_____

_____

_____

_____

_____

_____

_____

May 4

"And when the Chief Shepherd shall appear, ye shall receive a crown of glory that fadeth not away." 1 Peter 5:4

_____

_____

_____

_____

_____

_____

_____

_____

_____

_____

_____

_____

_____

_____

_____

_____

May 5

"The Lord will perfect that which concerneth me. Thy mercy, O Lord, endureth for ever;"

Psalm 138:8

_____

_____

_____

_____

_____

_____

_____

_____

_____

_____

_____

_____

_____

_____

_____

_____

May 6

"If we confess our sins, he is faithful and just to forgive us our sins,"   *1 John 1:9*

_____
_____
_____
_____
_____
_____
_____
_____
_____
_____
_____
_____
_____
_____
_____
_____
_____
_____
_____

May 7

"And I will give peace in the land, and ye shall lie down, and none shall make you afraid."

Leviticus 26:6

_____
_____
_____
_____
_____
_____
_____
_____
_____
_____
_____
_____
_____
_____
_____
_____
_____
_____

May 8

"For by grace are ye saved through faith;"

Ephesians 2:8

May 9

"Wait on the Lord; be of good courage, and He shall strengthen thine heart." — Psalm 27:14

May 10

"He that findeth his life shall lose it; and he that loseth his life for My sake shall find it." Matthew 10:39

May 11

"And this is the record, that God hath given to us eternal life, and this life is in His Son."   1 John 5:11

_____
_____
_____
_____
_____
_____
_____
_____
_____
_____
_____
_____
_____
_____
_____
_____
_____

May 12

". . . Thou shalt compass me about with songs of deliverance."

Psalm 32:7

_____
_____
_____
_____
_____
_____
_____
_____
_____
_____
_____
_____
_____
_____
_____
_____
_____
_____
_____
_____
_____
_____

May 13

"Now unto Him that is able to keep you from falling, and to present you faultless before the presence of His glory with exceeding joy,"   Jude 1:24

_____
_____
_____
_____
_____
_____
_____
_____
_____
_____
_____
_____
_____
_____
_____
_____
_____
_____
_____

May 14

"For I know the thoughts that I think toward you, saith the Lord, thoughts of peace, and not of evil…"

Jeremiah 29:11

_____
_____
_____
_____
_____
_____
_____
_____
_____
_____
_____
_____
_____
_____
_____
_____
_____
_____
_____
_____
_____

May 15

". . . For God cannot be tempted with evil, neither tempteth He any man . . ."   James 1:13

May 16

"I sought the Lord, and He heard me, and delivered me from all my fears."

Psalm 34:4

_____
_____
_____
_____
_____
_____
_____
_____
_____
_____
_____
_____
_____
_____
_____
_____
_____
_____
_____

May 17

"Nor height, nor depth, nor any other creature, shall be able to separate us from the love of God..."

Romans 8:39

_____
_____
_____
_____
_____
_____
_____
_____
_____
_____
_____
_____
_____
_____
_____
_____
_____
_____

May 18

"For the Lord thy God bringeth thee into a good land."

Deuteronomy 8:7

_____

_____

_____

_____

_____

_____

_____

_____

_____

_____

_____

_____

_____

_____

_____

_____

_____

May 19

"Love never faileth"

1 Corinthians 13:8

_____
_____
_____
_____
_____
_____
_____
_____
_____
_____
_____
_____
_____
_____
_____
_____
_____
_____

May 20

*". . . For whither thou goest, I will go;
and where thou lodgest, I will lodge, thy
people shall be my people, and thy God,
my God."* Ruth 1:16

_____
_____
_____
_____
_____
_____
_____
_____
_____
_____
_____
_____
_____
_____
_____
_____
_____
_____

May 21

"For Christ is the end of the law for righteousness to everyone that believeth."

Romans 10:4

_____
_____
_____
_____
_____
_____
_____
_____
_____
_____
_____
_____
_____
_____
_____
_____
_____

May 22

"And ye shall serve the Lord your God, and He shall bless thy bread, and thy water;" *Exodus 23:25*

_____
_____
_____
_____
_____
_____
_____
_____
_____
_____
_____
_____
_____
_____
_____
_____
_____
_____

May 23

"Your sorrow shall be turned into joy."
John 16:20

_____
_____
_____
_____
_____
_____
_____
_____
_____
_____
_____
_____
_____
_____
_____
_____
_____

May 24

"He will keep the feet of his saints..."
                                    1 Samuel 2:9

_____

_____

_____

_____

_____

_____

_____

_____

_____

_____

_____

_____

_____

_____

_____

_____

_____

May 25

"The sufferings of the present time are not worthy to be compared with the glory which shall be revealed in us."

Romans 8:18

May 26

"Better is little with the fear of the Lord than great treasure and trouble therewith."

Proverbs 15:16

_____

_____

_____

_____

_____

_____

_____

_____

_____

_____

_____

_____

_____

_____

_____

_____

_____

_____

_____

May 27

*"All scripture is given by inspiration
of God and is profitable."*

2 Timothy 3:16

_____

_____

_____

_____

_____

_____

_____

_____

_____

_____

_____

_____

_____

_____

_____

_____

_____

May 28

"Thou art my hiding place; thou shalt preserve me from trouble . . ."

Psalm 32:7

_____

_____

_____

_____

_____

_____

_____

_____

_____

_____

_____

_____

_____

_____

_____

_____

_____

_____

_____

_____

_____

May 29

*"There is therefore now no con-
demnation to them who are in
Christ Jesus."*   *Romans 8:1*

_____
_____
_____
_____
_____
_____
_____
_____
_____
_____
_____
_____
_____
_____
_____
_____
_____
_____
_____

May 30

"But whoso hearkeneth unto me shall dwell safely, and shall be quiet from fear of evil."

Proverbs 1:33

_____

_____

_____

_____

_____

_____

_____

_____

_____

_____

_____

_____

_____

_____

_____

_____

_____

_____

May 31

"...Eye hath not seen, nor ear heard...the things which God hath prepared for them that love Him."

1 Corinthians 2:9

_____

_____

_____

_____

_____

_____

_____

_____

_____

_____

_____

_____

_____

_____

_____

_____

June 1

"Draw nigh to God, and He will draw nigh to you." James 4:8

_____

_____

_____

_____

_____

_____

_____

_____

_____

_____

_____

_____

_____

_____

_____

_____

_____

_____

_____

June 2

"The grass withereth, the flower fadeth, but the word of our God shall stand for ever." Isaiah 40:8

_____

_____

_____

_____

_____

_____

_____

_____

_____

_____

_____

_____

_____

_____

_____

_____

_____

_____

June 3

"Nevertheless we, according to His promise, look for new heavens and a new earth, wherein dwelleth righteousness." 2 Peter 3:13

June 4

"Through God we shall do valiantly."

Psalm 60:12

_____
_____
_____
_____
_____
_____
_____
_____
_____
_____
_____
_____
_____
_____
_____
_____
_____
_____

June 5

". . . For we have heard Him ourselves, and know that this is indeed the Christ, the Saviour of the world." John 4:42

June 6

". . . The hand of our God is upon all them for good that seek him."

Ezra 8:22

June 7

"Rejoice, because your names are written in heaven."   *Luke 10:20*

_____

_____

_____

_____

_____

_____

_____

_____

_____

_____

_____

_____

_____

_____

_____

_____

_____

June 8

". . . Be not afraid, neither be thou dismayed; for the Lord thy God is with thee withersoever thou goest."

Joshua 1:9

June 9

"But ye shall receive power, after the Holy Ghost is come upon you;"

Acts 1:8

_____

_____

_____

_____

_____

_____

_____

_____

_____

_____

_____

_____

_____

_____

_____

_____

_____

June 10

"The Lord, before whom I walk, will send His angel with thee, and prosper thy way;"   *Genesis 24:40*

_____

_____

_____

_____

_____

_____

_____

_____

_____

_____

_____

_____

_____

_____

_____

_____

June 11

". . . Being justified by faith, we have peace with God through our Lord Jesus Christ." Romans 5:1

June 12

*"Delight thyself also in the Lord;
and He shall give thee the desires of
thine heart."*   *Psalm 37:4*

_____
_____
_____
_____
_____
_____
_____
_____
_____
_____
_____
_____
_____
_____
_____
_____
_____
_____

June 13

"When Christ, who is our life, shall appear, then shall ye also appear with Him in glory." Colossians 3:4

June 14

"The Lord, He is God in heaven above, and upon the earth beneath; there is none else." Deuteronomy 4:39

_____

_____

_____

_____

_____

_____

_____

_____

_____

_____

_____

_____

_____

_____

_____

June 15

"In Christ shall all be made alive."

1 Corinthians 15:22

June 16

"Many are the afflictions of the righteous; but the Lord delivereth him out of them all." Psalm 34:19

June 17

"With men it is impossible, but not with God; for with God all things are possible." *Mark 10:27*

June 18

"And all thy children shall be taught of the Lord; and great shall be the peace of thy children."

Isaiah 54:13

_____

_____

_____

_____

_____

_____

_____

_____

_____

_____

_____

_____

_____

_____

_____

_____

June 19

"The Lord knoweth how to deliver the godly out of temptations."

2 Peter 2:9

June 20

"Thou shalt make thy prayer unto him, and he shall hear thee . . ."

Job 22:27

_____
_____
_____
_____
_____
_____
_____
_____
_____
_____
_____
_____
_____
_____
_____
_____
_____

June 21

"It is your Father's good pleasure to give you the kingdom."

Luke 12:32

_____

_____

_____

_____

_____

_____

_____

_____

_____

_____

_____

_____

_____

_____

_____

_____

_____

_____

June 22

"I will make the wilderness a pool of water, and the dry land springs of water."   *Isaiah 41:18*

_____

_____

_____

_____

_____

_____

_____

_____

_____

_____

_____

_____

_____

_____

_____

_____

_____

_____

June 23

"Henceforth there is laid up for me a crown of righteousness, which the Lord, the righteous judge, shall give me at that day;"   *2 Timothy 4:8*

_____

_____

_____

_____

_____

_____

_____

_____

_____

_____

_____

_____

_____

_____

_____

_____

_____

June 24

"Thy word is a lamp unto my feet,
and a light unto my path."

Psalm 119:105

_____

_____

_____

_____

_____

_____

_____

_____

_____

_____

_____

_____

_____

_____

_____

_____

_____

June 25

"He being not a forgetful hearer, but a doer of the work, this man shall be blessed in his deed."

James 1:25

June 26

". . . Yet will he have compassion according to the multitude of his mercies."   *Lamentations 3:32*

_____
_____
_____
_____
_____
_____
_____
_____
_____
_____
_____
_____
_____
_____
_____
_____
_____

June 27

"He that is begotten of God keepeth himself, and that wicked one toucheth him not." *1 John 5:18*

_____
_____
_____
_____
_____
_____
_____
_____
_____
_____
_____
_____
_____
_____
_____
_____
_____
_____
_____

June 28

"The Lord is long suffering, and of great mercy, forgiving iniquity and transgression." Numbers 14:18

_____

_____

_____

_____

_____

_____

_____

_____

_____

_____

_____

_____

_____

_____

_____

_____

_____

June 29

"For all the law is fulfilled in one word, even in this; thou shalt love thy neighbor as thyself."

Galatians 5:14

June 30

"Be still, and know that I am God."
Psalm 46:10

_____

_____

_____

_____

_____

_____

_____

_____

_____

_____

_____

_____

_____

_____

_____

_____

_____

_____

July 1

"A good man obtaineth favour of the Lord."   *Proverbs 12:2*

_____

_____

_____

_____

_____

_____

_____

_____

_____

_____

_____

_____

_____

_____

_____

_____

_____

_____

July 2

". . . To an inheritance incorruptible, and undefiled, and that fadeth not away, reserved in heaven for you."

1 Peter 1:4

_____
_____
_____
_____
_____
_____
_____
_____
_____
_____
_____
_____
_____
_____
_____
_____
_____
_____

July 3

*"To him that soweth righteousness
shall be a sure reward."*

Proverbs 11:18

July 4

"And the peace of God, which passeth all understanding, shall keep your hearts and minds through Christ Jesus." *Philippians 4:7*

_____

_____

_____

_____

_____

_____

_____

_____

_____

_____

_____

_____

_____

_____

_____

_____

July 5

"For I will forgive their iniquity, and I will remember their sin no more." *Jeremiah 31:34*

_____

_____

_____

_____

_____

_____

_____

_____

_____

_____

_____

_____

_____

_____

_____

_____

_____

_____

_____

July 6

"But God is faithful, who will not suffer you to be tempted above that ye are able,"   *1 Corinthians 10:13*

_____
_____
_____
_____
_____
_____
_____
_____
_____
_____
_____
_____
_____
_____
_____
_____
_____

July 7

"For the Lord your God is gracious and merciful, and will not turn away his face from you, if ye return unto him."

2 Chronicles 30:9

_____

_____

_____

_____

_____

_____

_____

_____

_____

_____

_____

_____

_____

_____

_____

_____

_____

_____

_____

July 8

"But the God of all grace . . . after that ye have suffered a while, make you perfect, stablish, strengthen, settle you."   1 Peter 5:10

_____

_____

_____

_____

_____

_____

_____

_____

_____

_____

_____

_____

_____

_____

_____

_____

_____

_____

July 9

"The steps of a good man are ordered by the Lord, and He delighteth in his way."

_____
_____
_____
_____
_____
_____
_____
_____
_____
_____
_____
_____
_____
_____
_____
_____
_____
_____

July 10

"And the fruit of righteousness is sown in peace by them that make peace."

James 3:18

_____
_____
_____
_____
_____
_____
_____
_____
_____
_____
_____
_____
_____
_____
_____
_____

July 11

"Then shalt thou call, and the Lord shall answer."   *Isaiah 58:9*

July 12

"Blessed is the man that endureth temptation; for when he is tried, he shall receive the crown of life . . ."

James 1:12

July 13

" . . . A God ready to pardon, gracious and merciful, slow to anger, and of great kindness . . ."

Nehemiah 9:17

July 14

"Ye are all the children of light, and the children of the day."

1 Thessalonians 5:5

_____
_____
_____
_____
_____
_____
_____
_____
_____
_____
_____
_____
_____
_____
_____
_____

July 15

"But as truly as I live, all the earth shall be filled with the glory of the Lord."

Numbers 14:21

_____
_____
_____
_____
_____
_____
_____
_____
_____
_____
_____
_____
_____
_____
_____
_____
_____
_____
_____
_____

July 16

"But if ye be led of the Spirit, ye are not under the law."

Galatians 15:18

_____
_____
_____
_____
_____
_____
_____
_____
_____
_____
_____
_____
_____
_____
_____
_____
_____
_____

July 17

"A soft answer turneth away wrath . . ."   Proverbs 15:1

_____
_____
_____
_____
_____
_____
_____
_____
_____
_____
_____
_____
_____
_____
_____
_____
_____
_____
_____

July 18

"The Lord is not slack concerning His promise." 2 Peter 3:9

_____
_____
_____
_____
_____
_____
_____
_____
_____
_____
_____
_____
_____
_____
_____
_____
_____

July 19

"I, even I, am He that comforteth you . . ."

Isaiah 51:12

_____

_____

_____

_____

_____

_____

_____

_____

_____

_____

_____

_____

_____

_____

_____

_____

_____

_____

_____

July 20

"If ye abide in me, and my words abide in you, ye shall ask what ye will, and it shall be done unto you."

John 15:7

_____
_____
_____
_____
_____
_____
_____
_____
_____
_____
_____
_____
_____
_____
_____
_____
_____

July 21

"For I have satiated the weary soul, and I have replenished every sorrowful soul." *Jeremiah 31:25*

_____

_____

_____

_____

_____

_____

_____

_____

_____

_____

_____

_____

_____

_____

_____

_____

_____

_____

July 22

"Ye are God's husbandry, ye are God's building."   *1 Corinthians 3:9*

_____

_____

_____

_____

_____

_____

_____

_____

_____

_____

_____

_____

_____

_____

_____

_____

July 23

"And the Lord shall guide thee continually, and satisfy thy soul in drought."

Isaiah 58:11

July 24

"Being filled with the fruits of righteousness, which are by Jesus Christ, unto the glory and praise of God."
                              Philippians 1:11

_____

_____

_____

_____

_____

_____

_____

_____

_____

_____

_____

_____

_____

_____

_____

_____

July 25

"Whoso offereth praise glorifieth me"

Psalm 50:23

_____
_____
_____
_____
_____
_____
_____
_____
_____
_____
_____
_____
_____
_____
_____
_____
_____

July 26

"We do not cease to pray for you and to desire that ye might be filled with the knowledge of His will . . ."

Colossians 1:9

_____

_____

_____

_____

_____

_____

_____

_____

_____

_____

_____

_____

_____

_____

_____

_____

July 27

"How precious also are thy thoughts unto me, O God! How great is the sum of them!"

Psalm 139:17-18

_____

_____

_____

_____

_____

_____

_____

_____

_____

_____

_____

_____

_____

_____

_____

_____

July 28

". . . For ye are all one in Christ Jesus."

Galatians 3:28

_____

_____

_____

_____

_____

_____

_____

_____

_____

_____

_____

_____

_____

_____

_____

_____

_____

_____

July 29

"The Lord your God hath given you rest, and hath given you this land."

Joshua 1:13

_____

_____

_____

_____

_____

_____

_____

_____

_____

_____

_____

_____

_____

_____

_____

_____

_____

July 30

"Blessed be the God and Father of our Lord Jesus Christ, who hath blessed us with all spiritual blessings in heavenly places."

Ephesians 1:3

_____

_____

_____

_____

_____

_____

_____

_____

_____

_____

_____

_____

_____

_____

_____

_____

_____

July 31

"Acquaint now thyself with Him, and be at peace; thereby good shall come unto thee." Job 22:21

August 1

"And he said, My presence shall go with thee, and I will give thee rest."
Exodus 33:14

_____

_____

_____

_____

_____

_____

_____

_____

_____

_____

_____

_____

_____

_____

_____

_____

_____

August 2

"He that hath the Son hath life..."

1 John 5:12

_____

_____

_____

_____

_____

_____

_____

_____

_____

_____

_____

_____

_____

_____

_____

_____

_____

_____

_____

August 3

"The fear of the Lord prolongeth days . . ."
Proverbs 10:27

_____
_____
_____
_____
_____
_____
_____
_____
_____
_____
_____
_____
_____
_____
_____
_____
_____
_____

August 4

"According as his divine power hath given unto us all things that pertain unto life and godliness."

2 Peter 1:3

_____

_____

_____

_____

_____

_____

_____

_____

_____

_____

_____

_____

_____

_____

_____

_____

_____

_____

_____

August 5

"The Lord lift up his countenance upon thee, and give thee peace."

Numbers 6:26

_____

_____

_____

_____

_____

_____

_____

_____

_____

_____

_____

_____

_____

_____

_____

_____

August 6

"Verily, verily, I say unto you, if a man keep My saying, he shall never see death." John 8:51

August 7

"And I have put my words in thy mouth, and I have covered thee in the shadow of mine hand"

Isaiah 51:16

August 8

"Submit yourselves, therefore, to God. Resist the devil, and he will flee from you." James 4:7

_____
_____
_____
_____
_____
_____
_____
_____
_____
_____
_____
_____
_____
_____
_____
_____
_____

August 9

". . . To him that ordereth his conversation aright will I show the salvation of God."   *Psalm 50:23*

_____

_____

_____

_____

_____

_____

_____

_____

_____

_____

_____

_____

_____

_____

_____

August 10

". . . For blessed are they who keep my ways."
                                    Proverbs 8:32

August 11

"And he believed in the Lord; and he counted it to him for righteousness." Genesis 15:6

_____
_____
_____
_____
_____
_____
_____
_____
_____
_____
_____
_____
_____
_____
_____
_____
_____

August 12

"For there is one God, and one mediator between God and men, the man Christ Jesus,"

1 Timothy 2:5

_____
_____
_____
_____
_____
_____
_____
_____
_____
_____
_____
_____
_____
_____
_____
_____
_____
_____
_____
_____

August 13

"For the Lord your God is he who hath fought for you." Joshua 23:3

_____

_____

_____

_____

_____

_____

_____

_____

_____

_____

_____

_____

_____

_____

_____

August 14

"For this corruptible must put on incorruption, and this mortal must put on immortality."

1 Corinthians 15:53

_____
_____
_____
_____
_____
_____
_____
_____
_____
_____
_____
_____
_____
_____
_____
_____
_____
_____

August 15

"The Lord preserveth the faithful."

Psalm 31:23

_____
_____
_____
_____
_____
_____
_____
_____
_____
_____
_____
_____
_____
_____
_____
_____
_____
_____

August 16

"The words that I speak unto you,
they are spirit, and they are life."

John 6:63

August 17

"For the Lord God will help me; therefore shall I not be confounded."   *Isaiah 50:7*

_____

_____

_____

_____

_____

_____

_____

_____

_____

_____

_____

_____

_____

_____

_____

_____

August 18

"What things soever ye desire, when ye pray, believe that ye receive them, and ye shall have them." Mark 11:24

_____
_____
_____
_____
_____
_____
_____
_____
_____
_____
_____
_____
_____
_____
_____
_____

August 19

"And He shall bring forth thy righteousness as the light, and thy judgment as the noonday."

Psalm 37:6

_____

_____

_____

_____

_____

_____

_____

_____

_____

_____

_____

_____

_____

_____

_____

_____

_____

August 20

"The gift of God is eternal life."

Romans 6:23

_____

_____

_____

_____

_____

_____

_____

_____

_____

_____

_____

_____

_____

_____

_____

_____

_____

_____

August 21

"He hath remembered his covenant for ever, the word which he commanded to a thousand generations,"

August 22

"But as many as received him, to them gave he power to become the sons of God," John 1:12

August 23

"He healeth the broken in heart, and bindeth up their wounds."

Psalm 147:3

_____
_____
_____
_____
_____
_____
_____
_____
_____
_____
_____
_____
_____
_____
_____

_____

August 24

"I the Lord have called thee in righteousness, and will hold thine hand, and will keep thee . . ."

Isaiah 42:6

August 25

"Therefore if any man be in Christ, he is a new creature; old things are passed away; behold, all things are become new." *2 Corinthians 5:17*

_____

_____

_____

_____

_____

_____

_____

_____

_____

_____

_____

_____

_____

_____

_____

_____

August 26

"And it shall come to pass after-ward, that I will pour out my spirit upon all flesh; . . ." *Joel 2:28*

August 27

"Because thou hast kept the word of my patience, I also will keep thee from the hour of temptation."

Revelation 3:10

_____
_____
_____
_____
_____
_____
_____
_____
_____
_____
_____
_____
_____
_____
_____
_____
_____

August 28

"Fear thou not; for I am with thee. Be not dismayed; for I am thy God."

Isaiah 41:10

_____

_____

_____

_____

_____

_____

_____

_____

_____

_____

_____

_____

_____

_____

_____

_____

_____

_____

_____

August 29

"And whosoever liveth and believeth in Me shall never die."

John 11:26

August 30

"For I am the Lord, I change not; . . ."

Malachi 3:6

_____

_____

_____

_____

_____

_____

_____

_____

_____

_____

_____

_____

_____

_____

_____

_____

_____

_____

August 31

"For ye are all the children of God by faith in Christ Jesus."

Galatians 3:26

_____

_____

_____

_____

_____

_____

_____

_____

_____

_____

_____

_____

_____

_____

_____

_____

_____

_____

September 1

"And I will take sickness away from the midst of thee."

Exodus 23:25

_____
_____
_____
_____
_____
_____
_____
_____
_____
_____
_____
_____
_____
_____
_____
_____
_____
_____

September 2

"Blessed are the merciful; for they shall obtain mercy." Matthew 5:7

_____

_____

_____

_____

_____

_____

_____

_____

_____

_____

_____

_____

_____

_____

_____

September 3

"Though I walk in the midst of trouble, thou wilt revive me;"

Psalm 138:7

_____

_____

_____

_____

_____

_____

_____

_____

_____

_____

_____

_____

_____

_____

_____

_____

_____

_____

September 4

"For whatsoever is born of God overcometh the world;"

1 John 5:4

_____
_____
_____
_____
_____
_____
_____
_____
_____
_____
_____
_____
_____
_____
_____
_____
_____
_____

September 5

*"Commit thy works unto the
Lord, and thy thoughts shall be
established."*   *Proverbs 16:3*

_____

_____

_____

_____

_____

_____

_____

_____

_____

_____

_____

_____

_____

_____

_____

_____

_____

_____

_____

September 6

"But by the grace of God I am what I am"　　　　*1 Corinthians 15:10*

_____
_____
_____
_____
_____
_____
_____
_____
_____
_____
_____
_____
_____
_____
_____
_____
_____
_____

September 7

"Then they that feared the Lord spake often one to another; and the Lord hearkened, and heard it . . ."

Malachi 3:16

_____
_____
_____
_____
_____
_____
_____
_____
_____
_____
_____
_____
_____
_____
_____
_____
_____
_____
_____

September 8

"Stand fast therefore in the liberty wherewith Christ hath made us free,"

Galatians 5:1

_____

_____

_____

_____

_____

_____

_____

_____

_____

_____

_____

_____

_____

_____

_____

_____

_____

_____

September 9

". . . I have broken the bands of your yoke, and made you go upright."   *Leviticus 26:13*

_____

_____

_____

_____

_____

_____

_____

_____

_____

_____

_____

_____

_____

_____

_____

_____

_____

_____

September 10

"And account that the long-suffering of our Lord is salvation."

2 Peter 3:15

_____

_____

_____

_____

_____

_____

_____

_____

_____

_____

_____

_____

_____

_____

_____

_____

_____

September 11

"Though he fall, he shall not be utterly cast down; for the Lord upholdeth him with his hand."

Psalm 37:24

September 12

"For the Son of man is not come to destroy men's lives, but to save them." *Luke 9:56*

_____
_____
_____
_____
_____
_____
_____
_____
_____
_____
_____
_____
_____
_____
_____
_____
_____
_____

September 13

"There failed not aught of any good thing which the Lord had spoken unto the house of Israel; all came to pass." *Joshua 21:45*

September 14

"Humble yourselves in the sight of the Lord, and He shall lift you up."

James 4:10

_____

_____

_____

_____

_____

_____

_____

_____

_____

_____

_____

_____

_____

_____

_____

_____

_____

September 15

"I love them that love me; and those that seek me early shall find me."

Proverbs 8:17

_____
_____
_____
_____
_____
_____
_____
_____
_____
_____
_____
_____
_____
_____
_____
_____
_____
_____

September 16

"The word of the Lord endureth forever." 1 Peter 1:25

_____

_____

_____

_____

_____

_____

_____

_____

_____

_____

_____

_____

_____

_____

_____

_____

_____

September 17

"I will heal their backsliding, I will love them freely." *Hosea 14:4*

_____

_____

_____

_____

_____

_____

_____

_____

_____

_____

_____

_____

_____

_____

_____

_____

_____

_____

September 18

"Behold, I stand at the door, and knock; if any man hear My voice, and open the door, I will come in . . ."

Revelation 3:20

_____
_____
_____
_____
_____
_____
_____
_____
_____
_____
_____
_____
_____
_____
_____
_____
_____
_____

September 19

*"I am the Lord your God, and none
else; and my people shall never be
ashamed."*   *Joel 12:27*

_____
_____
_____
_____
_____
_____
_____
_____
_____
_____
_____
_____
_____
_____
_____
_____
_____
_____

September 20

"Wherefore thou art no more a servant, but a son; and if a son, then an heir of God through Christ."

Galatians 4:7

September 21

"For ye shall not go out with haste, nor go by flight; for the Lord shall go before you."   *Isaiah 52:12*

_____

_____

_____

_____

_____

_____

_____

_____

_____

_____

_____

_____

_____

_____

_____

_____

_____

September 22

*"Faithful is He that calleth you,
who also will do it."*

1 Thessalonians 5:24

_____
_____
_____
_____
_____
_____
_____
_____
_____
_____
_____
_____
_____
_____
_____
_____
_____

September 23

"But the salvation of the righteous is of the Lord; He is their strength in the time of trouble."   *Psalm 37:39*

_____

_____

_____

_____

_____

_____

_____

_____

_____

_____

_____

_____

_____

_____

_____

_____

_____

_____

_____

September 24

"He who soweth bountifully shall reap also bountifully."

2 Corinthians 9:6

_____

_____

_____

_____

_____

_____

_____

_____

_____

_____

_____

_____

_____

_____

_____

_____

_____

September 25

"He that giveth unto the poor shall not lack . . ."   *Proverbs 28:27*

September 26

"For this purpose the Son of God was manifested, that He might destroy the works of the devil."

1 John 3:8

_____

_____

_____

_____

_____

_____

_____

_____

_____

_____

_____

_____

_____

_____

_____

_____

_____

_____

September 27

"Fear not . . . I am thy shield, and thy exceeding great reward."

Genesis 15:1

_____
_____
_____
_____
_____
_____
_____
_____
_____
_____
_____
_____
_____
_____
_____
_____
_____
_____

September 28

"Ask, and it shall be given you; seek, and ye shall find; knock, and it shall be opened unto you;"

Matthew 7:7

_____

_____

_____

_____

_____

_____

_____

_____

_____

_____

_____

_____

_____

_____

_____

September 29

"They that sow in tears shall reap in joy."   *Psalm 126:5*

September 30

"Believe on the Lord Jesus Christ, and thou shalt be saved, and thy house."

Acts 16:31

October 1

"Cast thy burden upon the Lord, and He shall sustain thee; He shall never suffer the righteous to be moved."

Psalm 55:22

Deiorva Fuller   Neighbors son
B Stuy   Albert, join the
Kenny Vaust - rear driver   choir
pray 4 safety
Milton Taylor - Healing   Agusta Davis Edwards
mrs. Cleo Beard   doing better
mission trip 2 Kenya   with sickle
arrival, return safely
mission accomplished
Sallie Jackson -
directory
Eric McDowell
comfort care
alive
Pat Gibson
liver

October 2

"And all things, whatsoever ye shall ask in prayer, believing, ye shall receive." Matthew 21:22

_____
_____
_____
_____
_____
_____
_____
_____
_____
_____
_____
_____
_____
_____
_____
_____
_____

October 3

"I know that thou canst do every-thing, and that no thought can be withheld from thee." Job 42:2

October 4

". . . He who hath begun a good work in you will perform it until the day of Jesus Christ;"

Philippians 1:6

_____
_____
_____
_____
_____
_____
_____
_____
_____
_____
_____
_____
_____
_____
_____
_____
_____
_____

October 5

"He that hath pity upon the poor lendeth unto the Lord, and that which he hath given will He pay him again."

Proverbs 19:17

October 6

"The just shall live by faith."

Galatians 3:11

_____

_____

_____

_____

_____

_____

_____

_____

_____

_____

_____

_____

_____

_____

_____

_____

_____

_____

October 7

"I do set My bow in the cloud, and it shall be for a token of a covenant between me and the earth."

October 8

"Now the Lord is that Spirit; and where the Spirit of the Lord is, there is liberty."   2 Corinthians 3:17

_____
_____
_____
_____
_____
_____
_____
_____
_____
_____
_____
_____
_____
_____
_____
_____

October 9

"The Lord, thy God, in the midst of thee is mighty; He will save, He will rejoice over thee with joy;"

Zephaniah 3:17

October 10

"For we know that if our earthly house of this tabernacle were dissolved, we have a building of God, . . . eternal in the heavens."   *2 Corinthians 5:1*

_____
_____
_____
_____
_____
_____
_____
_____
_____
_____
_____
_____
_____
_____
_____
_____
_____
_____

October 11

"Behold, I am the Lord, the God of all flesh; is there anything too hard for Me?"

_____

_____
_____
_____
_____
_____
_____
_____
_____
_____
_____
_____
_____
_____
_____
_____
_____
_____
_____

October 12

"I am come a light into the world, that whosoever believeth on me should not abide in darkness."

John 12:46

_____

_____

_____

_____

_____

_____

_____

_____

_____

_____

_____

_____

_____

_____

_____

_____

October 13

"The angel of the Lord encampeth round about them that fear Him, and delivereth them." *Psalm 34:7*

_____
_____
_____
_____
_____
_____
_____
_____
_____
_____
_____
_____
_____
_____
_____
_____
_____

October 14

"In the world ye shall have tribulation: but be of good cheer; I have overcome the world."

John 16:33

_____

_____

_____

_____

_____

_____

_____

_____

_____

_____

_____

_____

_____

_____

_____

October 15

"And when I see the blood, I will pass over you, and the plague shall not be upon you to destroy you."

Exodus 12:13

_____
_____
_____
_____
_____
_____
_____
_____
_____
_____
_____
_____
_____
_____
_____
_____
_____
_____

October 16

"If any man will do His will, he shall know of the doctrine."

John 7:17

_____

_____

_____

_____

_____

_____

_____

_____

_____

_____

_____

_____

_____

_____

_____

_____

October 17

"Surely I will be with thee."

Judges 6:16

October 18

"Blessed are they that mourn; for they shall be comforted."

Matthew 5:4

_____

_____

_____

_____

_____

_____

_____

_____

_____

_____

_____

_____

_____

_____

October 19

"When thou walkest through the fire, thou shalt not be burned; neither shall the flame kindle upon thee."

Isaiah 43:2

_____
_____
_____
_____
_____
_____
_____
_____
_____
_____
_____
_____
_____
_____
_____
_____
_____
_____

October 20

"Take no thought how or what ye shall speak; for it shall be given you in that same hour what ye shall speak." *Matthew 10:19*

_____
_____
_____
_____
_____
_____
_____
_____
_____
_____
_____
_____
_____
_____
_____
_____

October 21

"By humility and the fear of the Lord are riches, and honor, and life."

Proverbs 22:4

_____

_____

_____

_____

_____

_____

_____

_____

_____

_____

_____

_____

_____

_____

_____

_____

_____

_____

October 22

"To him that overcometh will I give to eat of the hidden manna,"

_____
_____
_____
_____
_____
_____
_____
_____
_____
_____
_____
_____
_____
_____
_____
_____
_____
_____

October 23

"For as the heavens are high above the earth, so great is his mercy toward them that fear him."

Psalm 103:11

October 24

"But thanks be to God, who giveth us the victory through our Lord Jesus Christ."   *1 Corinthians 15:57*

_____
_____
_____
_____
_____
_____
_____
_____
_____
_____
_____
_____
_____
_____
_____
_____
_____
_____

October 25

"And it shall come to pass, that whosoever shall call on the name of the Lord shall be delivered."

Joel 2:32

October 26

"For God is not the author of confusion, but of peace . . ."

_____

_____

_____

_____

_____

_____

_____

_____

_____

_____

_____

_____

_____

_____

_____

_____

_____

October 27

". . . I will look unto the Lord; I will wait for the God of my salvation; my God will hear me." Micah 7:7

_____
_____
_____
_____
_____
_____
_____
_____
_____
_____
_____
_____
_____
_____
_____
_____
_____
_____
_____

October 28

"But where sin abounded, grace did much more abound."

Romans 5:20

_____

_____

_____

_____

_____

_____

_____

_____

_____

_____

_____

_____

_____

_____

_____

_____

_____

October 29

"But unto you that fear my name shall the Sun of righteousness arise with healing in his wings . . ."

Malachi 4:2

_____

_____

_____

_____

_____

_____

_____

_____

_____

_____

_____

_____

_____

_____

_____

_____

_____

_____

October 30

*"Peace I leave with you. My peace
I give unto you; not as the world
giveth, give I unto you."* John 14:27

_____
_____
_____
_____
_____
_____
_____
_____
_____
_____
_____
_____
_____
_____
_____
_____
_____

October 31

"It is God who girdeth me with strength, and maketh my way perfect."

Psalm 18:32

November 1

"The Lord is on my side; I will not fear; what can man do unto me?"

Psalm 118:6

_____

_____

_____

_____

_____

_____

_____

_____

_____

_____

_____

_____

_____

_____

_____

_____

_____

November 2

"Jesus saith unto him, I am the way, the truth, and the life; no man cometh unto the Father, but by me."

John 14:6

November 3

"And I will walk among you, and will be your God, and ye shall be my people."

Leviticus 26:12

_____

_____

_____

_____

_____

_____

_____

_____

_____

_____

_____

_____

_____

_____

_____

_____

_____

_____

November 4

"For ye are all the children of God by faith in Christ Jesus."

Galatians 3:26

_____

_____

_____

_____

_____

_____

_____

_____

_____

_____

_____

_____

_____

_____

_____

_____

_____

_____

_____

_____

November 5

"God shall send forth his mercy and his truth."   Psalm 57:3

_____

_____
_____
_____
_____
_____
_____
_____
_____
_____
_____
_____
_____
_____
_____
_____
_____
_____

November 6

"Who is he that overcometh the world, but he that believeth that Jesus is the Son of God?"

1 John 5:5

November 7

"Behold, the Lord's hand is not shortened, that it cannot save; neither His ear heavy, that it cannot hear."

Isaiah 59:1

_____
_____
_____
_____
_____
_____
_____
_____
_____
_____
_____
_____
_____
_____
_____
_____
_____
_____

November 8

"And such trust have we through Christ to Godward . . ."

2 Corinthians 3:4

_____

_____

_____

_____

_____

_____

_____

_____

_____

_____

_____

_____

_____

_____

_____

_____

_____

_____

_____

November 9

"... For the Lord your God, he it is that fighteth for you, as he hath promised you."

Joshua 23:10

_____

_____

_____

_____

_____

_____

_____

_____

_____

_____

_____

_____

_____

_____

_____

November 10

"Come unto me, all ye that labour and are heavy laden, and I will give you rest." *Matthew 11:28*

_____
_____
_____
_____
_____
_____
_____
_____
_____
_____
_____
_____
_____
_____
_____
_____
_____
_____

November 11

*"A thousand shall fall at thy side,
and ten thousand at thy right hand;
but it shall not come nigh thee."*

Psalm 91:7

_____
_____
_____
_____
_____
_____
_____
_____
_____
_____
_____
_____
_____
_____
_____
_____

November 12

"He that overcometh, the same shall be clothed in white raiment; and I will not blot out his name out of the book of life." Revelation 3:5

November 13

"I will command my blessing upon you."

Leviticus 25:21

November 14

"I, indeed, have baptized you with water, but He shall baptize you with the Holy Ghost." Mark 1:8

_____
_____
_____
_____
_____
_____
_____
_____
_____
_____
_____
_____
_____
_____
_____
_____
_____
_____
_____

November 15

"For the Lord shall be thy confidence, and shall keep thy foot from being taken." Proverbs 3:26

_____
_____
_____
_____
_____
_____
_____
_____
_____
_____
_____
_____
_____
_____
_____
_____

November 16

"And God shall wipe away all tears from their eyes; and there shall be no more death."

Revelation 21:4

_____

_____

_____

_____

_____

_____

_____

_____

_____

_____

_____

_____

_____

_____

_____

_____

_____

_____

November 17

". . . My kindness shall not depart from thee . . . saith the Lord who hath mercy on thee." *Isaiah 54:10*

_____
_____
_____
_____
_____
_____
_____
_____
_____
_____
_____
_____
_____
_____
_____
_____
_____
_____

November 18

"Know ye not that ye are the temple of God, and that the Spirit of God dwelleth in you?"

1 Corinthians 3:16

November 19

"Great peace have they who love thy law, and nothing shall offend them."　　　　Psalm 119:165

_____
_____
_____
_____
_____
_____
_____
_____
_____
_____
_____
_____
_____
_____
_____
_____
_____

November 20

"And ye shall know the truth, and the truth shall make you free."

John 8:32

_____

_____

_____

_____

_____

_____

_____

_____

_____

_____

_____

_____

_____

_____

_____

_____

_____

_____

November 21

"And the Lord shall help them, and deliver them; he shall deliver them from the wicked, and save them, because they trust in him."   *Psalm 37:40*

November 22

"Lo, I am with you always, even unto the end of the world."

Matthew 28:20

_____
_____
_____
_____
_____
_____
_____
_____
_____
_____
_____
_____
_____
_____
_____
_____
_____
_____
_____

November 23

"Trust in the Lord, and do good; so shalt thou dwell in the land, and verily thou shalt be fed."

November 24

"Said I not unto thee that, if thou wouldest believe, thou shouldest see the glory of God?"

John 11:40

_____

_____

_____

_____

_____

_____

_____

_____

_____

_____

_____

_____

_____

_____

_____

_____

_____

_____

November 25

"He maketh my feet like hinds' feet, and setteth me upon my high places."　　Psalm 18:33

_____
_____
_____
_____
_____
_____
_____
_____
_____
_____
_____
_____
_____
_____
_____
_____
_____
_____

November 26

"For the gifts and calling of God are without repentance."

Romans 11:29

_____
_____
_____
_____
_____
_____
_____
_____
_____
_____
_____
_____
_____
_____
_____
_____
_____
_____

November 27

"For He shall give His angels charge over thee, to keep thee in all thy ways."

Psalm 91:11

_____
_____
_____
_____
_____
_____
_____
_____
_____
_____
_____
_____
_____
_____
_____
_____
_____
_____

November 28

"The Lord shall deliver me from every evil work, and will preserve me unto His Heavenly Kingdom."

2 Timothy 4:18

November 29

"Hitherto hath the Lord helped us."

1 Samuel 7:12

_____
_____
_____
_____
_____
_____
_____
_____
_____
_____
_____
_____
_____
_____
_____
_____
_____
_____
_____

November 30

"The God of peace shall be with you."

_____
_____
_____
_____
_____
_____
_____
_____
_____
_____
_____
_____
_____
_____
_____
_____
_____
_____

December 1

"God sent his only begotten Son into the world, that we might live through him."

1 John 4:9

_____
_____
_____
_____
_____
_____
_____
_____
_____
_____
_____
_____
_____
_____
_____
_____
_____

December 2

"It is because of the Lord's mercies that we are not consumed, because his compassions fail not."

Lamentations 3:22

_____

_____

_____

_____

_____

_____

_____

_____

_____

_____

_____

_____

_____

_____

_____

_____

_____

_____

_____

December 3

"For ye were sometimes darkness, but now are ye light in the Lord."

Ephesians 5:8

December 4

"The Lord is the strength of my life;"

Psalm 27:1

_____
_____
_____
_____
_____
_____
_____
_____
_____
_____
_____
_____
_____
_____
_____
_____
_____
_____
_____

December 5

"Give, and it shall be given unto you;"

Luke 6:38

_____
_____
_____
_____
_____
_____
_____
_____
_____
_____
_____
_____
_____
_____
_____
_____
_____

December 6

"The meek shall inherit the earth, and shall delight themselves in the abundance of peace."   Psalm 37:11

_____

_____

_____

_____

_____

_____

_____

_____

_____

_____

_____

_____

_____

_____

_____

_____

_____

December 7

"For as many as are led by the Spirit of God, they are the sons of God."

Romans 8:14

_____
_____
_____
_____
_____
_____
_____
_____
_____
_____
_____
_____
_____
_____
_____
_____
_____

December 8

"The eternal God is thy refuge,"

Deuteronomy 33:27

_____

_____

_____

_____

_____

_____

_____

_____

_____

_____

_____

_____

_____

_____

_____

_____

_____

_____

_____

December 9

"Jesus Christ, the same yesterday, and today, and forever."

Hebrews 13:8

_____
_____
_____
_____
_____
_____
_____
_____
_____
_____
_____
_____
_____
_____
_____
_____
_____
_____

December 10

"His kingdom is an everlasting kingdom, and his dominion is from generation to generation."

Daniel 4:3

_____

_____

_____

_____

_____

_____

_____

_____

_____

_____

_____

_____

_____

_____

_____

_____

_____

_____

December 11

"For true and righteous are his judgments"   *Revelations 19:2*

_____
_____
_____
_____
_____
_____
_____
_____
_____
_____
_____
_____
_____
_____
_____
_____
_____
_____

December 12

"For the Lord giveth wisdom; out of his mouth cometh knowledge and understanding."　　*Proverbs 2:6*

December 13

"I can do all things through Christ, who strengtheneth me."

Philippians 4:13

_____

_____

_____

_____

_____

_____

_____

_____

_____

_____

_____

_____

_____

_____

_____

_____

_____

_____

December 14

"He that believeth and is baptized shall be saved;"   Mark 16:16

_____

_____

_____

_____

_____

_____

_____

_____

_____

_____

_____

_____

_____

_____

_____

_____

_____

_____

December 15

"If ye be willing and obedient, ye shall eat the good of the land."

Isaiah 1:19

_____
_____
_____
_____
_____
_____
_____
_____
_____
_____
_____
_____
_____
_____
_____
_____
_____

December 16

"Blessed is he that readeth . . . and keeps those things which are written therein; for the time is at hand."

Revelation 1:3

_____
_____
_____
_____
_____
_____
_____
_____
_____
_____
_____
_____
_____
_____
_____
_____
_____
_____

December 17

"And blessed is he, whosoever shall not be offended in me."

Luke 7:23

_____

_____

_____

_____

_____

_____

_____

_____

_____

_____

_____

_____

_____

_____

_____

_____

_____

December 18

"The upright shall dwell in thy presence."　　　*Psalm 140:13*

_____
_____
_____
_____
_____
_____
_____
_____
_____
_____
_____
_____
_____
_____
_____
_____
_____
_____

December 19

"But the Lord is faithful, who shall stablish you, and keep you from evil."

2 Thessalonians 3:3

_____

_____

_____

_____

_____

_____

_____

_____

_____

_____

_____

_____

_____

_____

_____

_____

_____

December 20

"Our God shall fight for us."

Nehemiah 4:20

_____

_____

_____

_____

_____

_____

_____

_____

_____

_____

_____

_____

_____

_____

_____

_____

_____

_____

December 21

"Blessed are they that hear the word of God, and keep it."

Luke 11:28

_____

_____

_____

_____

_____

_____

_____

_____

_____

_____

_____

_____

_____

_____

_____

_____

December 22

"Some trust in chariots, and some in horses; but we will remember the name of the Lord our God."

December 23

"But unto every one of us is given grace according to the measure of the gift of Christ."   Ephesians 4:7

_____
_____
_____
_____
_____
_____
_____
_____
_____
_____
_____
_____
_____
_____
_____
_____
_____

December 24

"For unto us a child is born, unto us a son is given,"   *Isaiah 9:6*

_____

_____

_____

_____

_____

_____

_____

_____

_____

_____

_____

_____

_____

_____

_____

_____

_____

December 25

"I am come that they might have life"

_____
_____
_____
_____
_____
_____
_____
_____
_____
_____
_____
_____
_____
_____
_____
_____
_____
_____

December 26

"The Lord thy God, he it is who doth go with thee; he will not fail thee, nor forsake thee."

Deuteronomy 31:6

_____
_____
_____
_____
_____
_____
_____
_____
_____
_____
_____
_____
_____
_____
_____
_____
_____
_____
_____

December 27

"For with God nothing shall be impossible." *Luke 1:37*

_____

_____

_____

_____

_____

_____

_____

_____

_____

_____

_____

_____

_____

_____

_____

_____

_____

December 28

"He shall cover thee with his feathers, and under his wings shalt thou trust; his truth shall be thy shield and buckler." *Psalm 91:4*

December 29

"If thou canst believe, all things are possible to him that believeth."

Mark 9:23

_____

_____

_____

_____

_____

_____

_____

_____

_____

_____

_____

_____

_____

_____

_____

_____

_____

_____

December 30

"In all thy ways acknowledge him, and he shall direct thy paths."

Proverbs 3:6

December 31

"Allelujah! For the Lord God omnipotent reigneth."

Revelation 19:6